HOW TO SWEAR
AROUND THE WORLD

HOW TO SWEAR

AROUND THE WORLD

BY JASON SACHER

ILLUSTRATIONS BY TOBY TRIUMPH

CHRONICLE BOOKS

SAN FRANCISCO

Copyright © 2012 by Chronicle Books LLC.
Illustrations copyright © 2012 by Toby Triumph.
All rights reserved. No part of this book may be reproduced
in any form without written permission from the publisher.

Library of Congress Cataloging-in-Publication Data
How to swear around the world.
    p. cm.
 ISBN 978-1-4521-1087-5
 1. Words, Obscene. I. Chronicle Books (Firm)

 P410.O27H69 2012
 417'.2--dc23

                        2011051361

Manufactured in China
Text by Jason Sacher.
Designed by Alexandra Styc.

10 9 8 7 6 5 4 3

Chronicle Books LLC
680 Second Street
San Francisco, California 94107
www.chroniclebooks.com

INTRODUCTION

LET'S ALL BE HONEST: IF YOU SPEAK, YOU SWEAR. Simple as that. Linguists postulate that the average person uses "taboo" words roughly eighty to ninety times each day, and have recorded swearing in children as young as twelve months. If you multiply those eighty swears a day by the six billion-plus people on the planet, well, that's a lot of swearing; it's a veritable shitload.

This book is intended to give you an overview of that shitload—the rich and effulgent stream of profanity, insults, put-downs, metaphors, and trash-talking that breathes life into language and adds some much-needed salt to all our varied communications. From the playground to parliament to the used car lot, swear words, cursing, oaths, and coarse language (whatever you choose to call it) help us signify our intent, win arguments, tell jokes, and ease (or cause) awkward situations. As Carl Sandburg said of slang, swear words are language with its sleeves rolled up, ready to do business.

With over six thousand different languages spoken on the planet, this is by no means a comprehensive catalog of all the various ways one can offend with words, but we've done our best to get you from one corner of the globe to the other with a host of useful profane utterances and offensive oaths. Broadly speaking, swear words are a great leveler. You'll discover that subjects that tend to offend in Illinois will probably do the same in Austria or Singapore, with slight tweaks for social mores along the way.

The common ground of swearing—its universal nature from culture to culture—should give us hope for the future. We are the same: we all say fuck! shit! and asshole! although we pronounce them differently and they might mean slightly different things from one speaker to the next.

Every language possesses creative ways to defame someone's mother, tell people they were raised by animals, and describe the various substances and fluids that usher forth from our bodies. As a species, we are also well-stocked with those harder-to-translate insults and idiomatic expressions that turn swearing into true poetry. *How to Swear Around the World* is here to help you unleash your profane poet laureate, with an international glossary of the world's most offensive slurs. Keep it in your back pocket and you'll always have something handy to yell when someone cuts you off in traffic in Osaka *(Bakayaro!)* or you drop your passport into the Seine *(Quel bordel!)*.

Given the title of this book, it should go without saying that the language cataloged herein is offensive, and will be offensive to those who happen to hear it, even if it doesn't sound offensive to you. For instance, calling someone a "turtle" in English will probably cause head-scratching rather than the flying fists towards your face that would ensue in parts of China. Similarly, be wary of insulting a man's moustache in many Arabic countries or comparing a Persian-speaking person to a donkey. In fact, just BE WARY. Every phrase in this book is bound to insult, annoy, or inflame those who hear it, and can get you punched, deported, or worse. Remember, it's always best to swear with caution.

But also: swear with joy. You're a human being; it's your birthright.

Chapter One

THE
MOTHERLODE

⚬⚬⚬

GLOBALLY SPEAKING, no matter what she may have done to you over the course of your life, we tend to take offense when somebody speaks ill of our mother. Every culture has its own version of the standard mother insults, most of which imply that the mother in question is employed as a streetwalker, engages in sexual intercourse with animals or random strangers, or is—generally speaking—a woman of loose morals and low character.

Despite the frequency with which these oaths occur, their power to offend remains quite strong—things get ugly fast when you defame dear old mom. In many cultures, however, the "mother" vulgarities described in the following pages are more often used as interjections and exclamations—providing an outlet for everything from the pain of a stubbed toe to anger over a tax audit or a bad call from a football ref.

What it comes down to is that mother insults, like mothers themselves, are incredibly versatile. The skilled curser can use them jovially amongst friends, or to convey extreme anger at a person (towards a drunken man who spills his beer on you, for instance) or a situation (such as you, drunk, spilling your beer on someone). From "Mamma mia" to "Mother flipper!" let's hope the world's mothers are proud of how frequently and creatively we bandy their name about.

$#@*! $#@*! #$@%! *#@$! $#@! $#@*! $#@! $#@! @#$*! $#@*! $#@! $#@*!

$#@! YOUR MOTHER

There's an old Hebrew proverb, "God cannot be everywhere, so he created mothers." As long as this remains the case, the commonality of motherfucks! and fuck your mothers! will be unceasing. Fraught with Freudian overtones as it is, this utilitarian insult packs a lot of bang for its buck.

Use it to express extreme displeasure:

FRENCH
Nique ta mère! Je suis tombé dans l'escalier!
"Fuck your mother! I have fallen down the stairs!"

Or hurl it as an insult:

SPANISH
¡Que me empujó por las escaleras! ¡Chinga tu madre!
"You pushed me down the stairs! Fuck your mother!"

As we see from the chart below, it works quite well on its own as well.

LANGUAGE	*"Fuck your mother!"*
AFRIKAANS	*Fok jou ma!*
ALBANIAN	*Ta qifsha nanen!*
ARABIC	*Nikomak!*
BASQUE	*Cogida zure ama!*
BULGARIAN	*Mama ti daba!*
BURMESE	*Minn may minn lo!*

LANGUAGE	*"Fuck your mother!"*
CHINESE (CANTONESE)	*D'iu ne lo mo!*
CHINESE (MANDARIN)	*Tsao ni ma!*
CZECH	*Kurva svou matku!*
DUTCH	*Ik neuk je moeder!*
ESTONIAN	*Kurat su ema!*
FINNISH	*Vittu teidän äiti!*
FRENCH	*Nique ta mère!*
GERMAN	*Fick deine Mutter!*
GREEK	*Gamo ti mana sou!*
HEBREW	*Koos emek!*
HUNGARIAN	*Fasz az anyád!*
ICELANDIC	*Ríða móður þinni!*
ITALIAN	*Scopa tua mamma!*
JAVANESE	*Itil'e mbokmu!*
MALAYSIAN	*Kongkek mak kau!*
NORWEGIAN	*Gå å knull morra de!*
RUSSIAN	*Yehbu tvoyu mat!*
SLOVENIAN	*Ebi svojo mamo!*
SPANISH	*¡Tu puta madre!*
SPANISH (MEXICO/AMERICAS)	*¡Chinga tu madre!*
SWAHILI	*Kuma mamako!*
TAGALOG	*Kingina!*
TURKISH	*Anani sikerim!*
VIETNAMESE (NORTHERN)	*Địt mẹ mày!*
VIETNAMESE (SOUTHERN)	*Đụ má mày!*

YOUR MOTHER'S CHOICE OF EMPLOYMENT

⌒⌒

Mothers today hold very impressive jobs all over the world. Some are doctors, some are lawyers, some are prime ministers. In the world of profanity, however, they are all prostitutes. With varying shifts of tone from culture to culture, the following insults all amount to informing someone that their mother is either a working girl or extremely liberal with her sexual partners. Not at all subtle, these insults should only be used when you wish to cause great offense.

"Your mother is a whore!"

ARABIC
Mook kebba!

CZECH
Tvoje matka je kurva!

DANISH
Din mor ligner en luder!

DUTCH
Hoerenjong!
("Whore-son!")

FRENCH
Ta mère la pute!

GERMAN
Deine Mutter ist eine Hure!

GREEK
I mana sou ine putana!

HUNGARIAN
Anyád egy kurva!

ITALIAN
Tua madre è puttana!

KOREAN
Um chang se kki!

NORWEGIAN
Morra di er hore!

PERSIAN
Madar jendeh!

$#@!

Fudge Your Mother!

Kurwa (whore) is an extremely common swear word in Poland, used as an interjection the way English speakers use "damn" and "shit." More refined speakers, perhaps feeling the word is a little impolite, have developed euphemistic derivatives of *kurwa* (like saying "darn" or "shoot" instead of "damn" and "shit") including *kurcze* and *kurde*. You can say the nonsensical phrase *Kurce twoja mac´!* if your aim is to be as polite as possible with your impolite phrase.

POLISH
Kurwa twoja mać!

SPANISH
¡Tu puta madre!

TAGALOG
Tang ina mo!

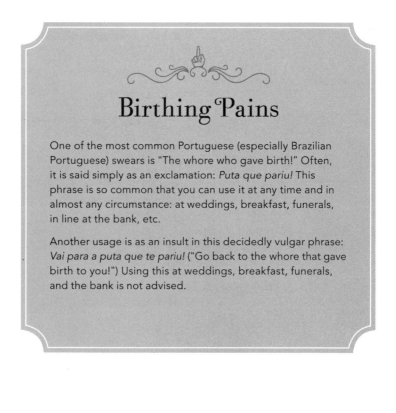

Birthing Pains

One of the most common Portuguese (especially Brazilian Portuguese) swears is "The whore who gave birth!" Often, it is said simply as an exclamation: *Puta que pariu!* This phrase is so common that you can use it at any time and in almost any circumstance: at weddings, breakfast, funerals, in line at the bank, etc.

Another usage is as an insult in this decidedly vulgar phrase: *Vai para a puta que te pariu!* ("Go back to the whore that gave birth to you!") Using this at weddings, breakfast, funerals, and the bank is not advised.

YOUR MOTHER AND HER RELATION TO THE ANIMAL KINGDOM

Old MacDonald had a farm, and on that farm he had a truly filthy mouth. When it's time to really insult someone's mother, cultures all over the world invoke the barnyard. With a "Your mother's a cow" here, and a "Your mother's a turtle" there, here a dog, there a donkey, everywhere a pig pig, there is no shortage of animal insults to choose from. The following are a few of our favorites.

ARABIC
Ibn il-labwa!
"Son of a lioness!"

FRENCH
Ta mère est une vache.
"Your mother is a cow."

GERMAN
Saubua!
"Son of a pig!"

HINDI
Ullu ke pathe!
"You are born of an owl!"

ITALIAN
Tua madre è un porco.
"Your mother is a pig."

KOREAN
Kotchu sekki!
"You are the son of a penis!"

We include this here since identifying one's mother as a body part is just as bad as calling her an animal.

PERSIAN
Mardar sag.
"Your mother is a dog."

TURKISH
Annen bir inek.
"Your mother is a cow."

Eşşoğlu eşek!
"You are born of a donkey!"

WELSH
Eich mam A yw A hen sguthan!
"Your mother is an old wood pigeon!"

TURTLES AND TURTLE EGGS:

A Cross-Cultural Education in Crassness

CHINESE (MANDARIN)
Nide muchin shr ega da wukwei.
"Your mother is a giant freshwater turtle."

By calling an enemy's mother a turtle, you're implying that she is sexually promiscuous, and that her offspring are illegitimate. This colorful expression dates back a thousand years to the Song dynasty, arising from the fact that the head of a turtle as it emerges from its shell resembles a penis.

Another common derogatory term is *wángbadàn* which literally translates as "turtle egg," implying "son of a whore/bitch." *Wángbādàn* is often shortened to *wángbā*.

YOUR MOTHER AND HER RELATIONS WITH THE ANIMAL KINGDOM

Perhaps even harsher than implying that someone's mother is not a human being, there are many ways to say that the mother in question happily copulates with animals in her spare time. It paints a quick and mean-spirited picture.

These curses should truly be reserved for moments of extreme anger. We as a species do not take kindly to the mental images that the phrases below conjure. As you can imagine, dogs are the most obvious globally insulting animal of choice to pair with a mother, but certain cultures have fun throwing a few more culturally specific animals in there, consider the bears in Bulgaria, and reindeer (of course!) in Finland.

BULGARIAN
Mayka ti duha na mechki v gorata.
"Your mother performs oral sex upon bears in the forest."

DUTCH
Zoon van een hoerige kameel!
"Son of a camel whore!"
> With this insult, it's unclear whether one is saying the mother in question was a camel that was also a prostitute or a prostitute who serviced camels.

FINNISH
Äitisi nai poroja!
"Your mother copulates with reindeer!"

LAOTIAN
Ma see mea mung!
"Your mother enjoys keeping intimate company with dogs!"

POLISH

Twoja stara ciagnie psu.

"Your mother engages in carnal activities with dogs."

RUSSIAN

Pyos yob tvoyu mat!

"A male dog had sex with your mother!"

Kor-rovie khuy-ee!

"Your mother makes it with cows!"

SERBIAN

Jebo ti pas mater!

"May your mother have intimate relations with dogs!"

ARTFULLY CURSING YOUR MOTHER
Part 1: Mild

∽

The world of swearing is an endlessly evolving mix of new terms, fresh innuendoes, and energetic put-downs. Any artful curser will tell you that sometimes, coming right out and saying "Your mother is a whore" or "Your mother is fat" or "Your mother is ugly" isn't nearly as effective as something like, "Your mother willingly grows hair on her face," or "Your mother is anatomically unable to urinate like other members of her gender!"

None of the phrases that follow are particularly nice things to say, but this section contains some slightly milder, slightly more interesting way of defaming a mother.

BULGARIAN
Mayka ti pikae prava!
"Your mother pees standing up!"

CHINESE (CANTONESE)
Le lo mo yau so!
"Your mother has a beard!"

HEBREW
Koos emek!
"Your mother's nether regions!"

A Hebrew oath borrowed from the Arabic, this phrase is quite prevalent on the streets of Israel, where it is used as an angry interjection.

ITALIAN
Tua madre si da per niente!
"Your mother gives it away for free!"

MALAYALAM (INDIA)
Parrayande mone!
"Son of a pariah!"

Parrayande mole!
"Daughter of a pariah!"

> In class-conscious Mayalam, to call someone the son or daughter of a pariah is extremely offensive.

SWAHILI
Mama yako ni oban!
"Your mother is a dirty old witch!"

TAMIL (INDIA)
Gumbal ku porandavaney!
"Son of a crowd!"

Virundali ku porandavaney!
"Son of a guest!"

> In the Tamil language of southern India, you can imply the object of your insult has a mother with loose morals by questioning his or her paternity.

ARTFULLY CURSING YOUR MOTHER
Part 2: Offensive

Sometimes there's no sense in beating around the bush. When your sole aim is to offend and insult, the mother curses below will get the job done. Featuring prostitution, blasphemy, necrophilia, and fecal incontinence, sometimes combined in a single phrase, these insults are not for amateurs, and should only be deployed by expert multi-taskers and swearing connoisseurs.

Scatological

SPANISH
¡Me cago en tu puta madre!
"I defecate upon your prostitute mother!"

Religious

HUNGARIAN
Az Isten bassza meg a büdös rücskös kurva anyádat!
"May God fornicate with your whore mother!"

Political

KOREAN
Ni me shi me nuhn il bon chon haam ey soo yong het nuhn dae.
"Your mother swam out to meet the Japanese battleships."
    The implication here is that not only is the mother in question a
    capitulator to an invading army, but she is also an eager prostitute.

Morbid

ROMANIAN
Futu-tzi coliva ma~tii!
"Screw your mother's funeral meal!"

Bizarre

ARABIC
Eyreh be afass seder emmak!
"A dick in your mother's ribcage!"

Vulgar and Impossible

SPANISH
¡La reputisima madre que te remil pario!
"The whore that gave birth to you bore a thousand children!"

Demonic

SWEDISH
Din mamma är ful och din pappa är ondskan själv!
"Your mother is ugly, and your father is evil incarnate!"

Bizarre and Morbid

ROMANIAN
Futu-ți morții mă-tii!
"Fuck your mother's dead ancestors!"

Necrophiliac

BOSNIAN
Jebem li ti mrtvu majku!
"I fuck your dead mother!"

YOUR UNCLE, YOUR SISTER, YOUR GRANDFATHER, YOUR MOTHER-IN-LAW

Mothers are not alone in having their virtue besmirched. When it comes to insults, apparently, the whore apple doesn't fall far from the prostitute tree. Research shows that the aunt is the preferred relative to defame, but brothers, sisters, and uncles take their share of abuse as well. Use these phrases when rudeness is called for but disparaging someone's mother is a little too harsh.

Aunts

BULGARIAN
Pichkata lelina!
"Your aunt's nether regions!"

FRENCH
Votre tante est pute!
"Your aunt is a whore!"

HINDI
ACP.
> *ACP* stands for "Aunty come please." In Hindi slang, the English word "Aunty" has come to have the same meaning that MILF does in English—that is, an older attractive female.

PORTUGUESE
A puta da tua tia!
"Your aunt is a whore!"

RUSSIAN
Vashi tetki kiska!
"Your aunt's nether regions!"

Uncles

ICELANDIC
Frandseroir!
"Uncle-fucker!"

Sisters

HEBREW
Achotcha be geves!
"Your sister into the gypsum!"
> This implies a sister being used as drywall or plaster—
> the implication being that she would be quite dead.

HINDI
Bahen ke takke!
"Sister's balls!"

Bhen chhod bhaynchod!
"Sister-fucker!"

Fathers

FIJIAN
Maqai tamamu!
"Fuck your father!"

ITALIAN
Figlio de papa!
"Papa's boy!"

Grandparents

BULGARIAN
Shte ti go tura na babati!
"Fuck your grandmother!"

CHINESE (MANDARIN)
Tsao ni lao lao!
"Fuck your grandmother!"

ICELANDIC
Afatottari!
"Grandfather-fucker!"

WELSH
Dos i chwarae efo dy nain!
"Go fuck your granny!"

The Family as a Whole

CHINESE (MANDARIN)
Tsao ni zu zong shi ba dai!
"Fuck the eighteen generations of your ancestors!"

ITALIAN
Li mortacci tua!
"[A fucking] upon your dishonored dead relatives!"

Chapter Two

EVERYDAY OATHS
AND EXCLAMATIONS

⸻

T's THE LITTLE THINGS toward which most of our swearing is directed. The day-to-day insults that life throws our way, we meet with day-to-day curses—no less vulgar for how often we use them. The words charted below range in strength from the equivalent of "Oh, for fuck's sake!" to a more vanilla "Gosh darn it!" but all of them add rich texture to everyday language.

Just as an apprentice chef needs to learn the subtleties of seasoning and spices, it takes years of study to be able to grasp the intricacies of some of these curses and learn how to apply them properly in a variety of situations. Study them now, and soon you'll be flavoring your swears with a *soupçon* of screw-you, a sprinkle of fuck-my-life, and a dash of go-to-hell. Salty!

$#@*! $#@*! #$@%! *#@$! $#@! $#@*! $#@! $#@! @#$*! $#@*! $#@! $#@*!

SWEARING IN THE FACE OF LIFE'S DAILY DISASTERS

Day after day, night after night, life presents us with endless reasons to curse, exclaim, and yell—either in pain or pleasure. We don't always say the smartest or most clever phrases in those heated moments, when our poetic nature tends to get lost in a sea of damns, hells, christs, and craps. These swears may not be lyrical, but they get the damn job done, hell yeah they do.

Various Damns

CHINESE (CANTONESE)
Yiu!
"Damn it!"

DUTCH
God verdomme!
"God damn it!"

GERMAN
Verdammt nochmal!
"Damn it all to hell!"

ICELANDIC
Anzvíti!
"Damn!"

PORTUGUESE
Porra!
"Damn!"

SPANISH
¡Maldicion!
"Damn!"

TURKISH
Lanet olsun!
"Damn it!"

Various Craps

(For more scatological insults, see Global Scatology 101 and Naughty Bits, page 115.)

ARABIC
Akh laa!
"Oh crap!"

CHINESE (MANDARIN)
Da bien!
"Oh shit!"

JAPANESE
Mazui!
"Oh crap!"

RUSSIAN
Khu-YA-sye!
"Holy shit!"

TAGALOG
Buwisét!
"Oh crap!"

THAI
Chip haai la!
"Oh crap!"

YIDDISH
A chorbn!
"What a crappy mess!"

Various Hells and Others

FRENCH (CANADIAN)
Crisse de Tabernak!
"Jesus fucking Christ!"

HEBREW
Ben zona!
"Son of a bitch!"
> Most often used as an expression of dismay rather than an insult.

IRISH
Ifreann na fola!
"Bloody hell!"

KOREAN
Woot gi ji ma!
"Whatever!"

POLISH
Zajebisty! (zai-eb-isteh)
"Fan-fucking-tastic!"
> Can be used in jest or to truly mean fantastic.

SPANISH (MEXICO)
¡Hijole!
"Holy smokes!"

CAZZO!

For Italians, *Cazzo! Is* the holy grail of swear words. The closest translation is "cock" (the body part), but cazzo has long since transcended its definition. Profane, silly, and with a level of vulgarity that shifts according to its usage, *cazzo* is truly a curse built for everyday use.

Used on its own as in interjection, *Cazzo!* has about the same strength as uttering "Oh shit!"

Cazzo is also used in an almost endless string of colorful expressions and phrases:

Che cazzo fai?
"What the dick are you doing?"

Che cazzo vuoi?
"What the dick do you want?"

Col cazzo!
"The cocks!"
> This interjection is often used as a contradiction, sort of similar to "My arse!" in UK English or "Bullshit!" in American English.

Fatti i cazzi tuoi!
"Mind your own dicks!"

Alla cazzo
> A shortened version of a *cazzo di cane,* "the way of the dog's dick." To do something *alla cazzo* is do it in an ass-backward way.

Cazzi acidi!

"Sour dicks!"

> Big trouble, the equivalent of being in deep shit.

Frega un cazzo!

"I don't give a dick!"

Testa di cazzo!

"Dickhead!"

> As in "You're a dickhead!"(*Sei una testa di cazzo!*) or "Apologies!
> I'm a dickhead!" (*Scuse! Sono una testa di cazzo!*)

Grazie al cazzo!

"Thanks to the dick!"

> Sort of the equivalent of saying "No shit, Sherlock!" when
> something is obvious and doesn't need further explanation.

PERKELE

The most renowned curse word in Finnish is *perkele*.

Perkele was originally the name of a pre-Christian Finnish thunder God, but over the centuries came to mean any demon or devil and eventually became a common swear word. Like the Italian *cazzo*, *perkele* is a multifaceted word, used as an insult, an interjection, or a joyful exclamation.

Upset

Perkele!
"Ah shit!"

> Note: Finns tend to draw out and roll their r's when saying *perkele*. So: *"Perrrrrrrrrkele!"*

Joyful

Perkele! Me voitimme!
"Holy crap, we won!"

Truly Angry

Perkele vittu saatana!
"Fuck the devil, Satan!"

Insulting

Sika perkele!
"You fucking devil pig!"

CONS

As far as everyday curses are concerned, the go-to word for French speakers is, without a doubt, *con* (and its variations and derivatives). It's frequently noted that most tourists first encounter *Con!* when it's shouted by Parisian taxi drivers. *Con's* dictionary definition is a derogatory term for female genitalia, but as we've seen with *perkele* and *cazzo, con* has long since left behind its original meaning. *Con's* utter ubiquity has softened its tone to mean roughly asshole, schmuck, or dumb-ass.

It can be used as an expression of frustration:
Ne fais pas le con!
"Don't be such a silly wanker!"

Or in serious anger at someone's actions:
Ne me prenez pas pour un con!
"Don't take me for an asshole!"

Or as an exclamation of disbelief:
C'est des conneries!
"This is bullshit!"

Related to con are the terms *conard* and *connasse. Conard* is the masculine version and means "bastard," and *connasse,* the feminine, means "bitch."

Quel conard!
"What a bastard!"

Quelle connasse!
"What a bitch!"

Many beginning French speakers can get themselves into hot water confusing *conard* (bastard) with *canard* (duck).

More Cons

To express dissatisfaction:
C'est à la con!
"This is worthless!"

To convey that someone is extremely stupid:
Tu es con comme un balai!
"You are as stupid as a broom!"

Tu es con à bouffer de la bite!
"You stupid dickhead!"

To strongly express your lack of interest:
Je me contrefous de ce que tu penses!
"I don't give a fuck what you think!"

BROTHELS

༄

The phrase "What a brothel!" is surprisingly international. Used in a variety of European cultures, it's a colorful way to express frustration with an unpleasant situation, total mess, or screw-up. If you loan your friend your car and he crashes it into a tree, this is a "brothel." If the line at airport security is monstrously long and you're running late for a flight, this too would be a brothel. You might also exclaim "What a brothel!" if you find yourself in an establishment where people pay women to have intercourse with them.

CZECH
Bordel!
  Borrowed from the French.

FRENCH
Quel bordel!
Bordel de merde!
  "Brothel of shit" is the equivalent of saying "damn it to hell!"

ITALIAN
Che casino!
  Italians also have the nouns *casinaro* (m) and *casinista* (f) as a way to label someone a troublemaker.

RUSSIAN
Bardák!

SWEDISH
Bordell!

CARRION, HORSERADISH, AND WOUNDS: COLORFUL OATHS FROM AROUND THE WORLD

∽

The collection of terms below are approved for everyday use—they're mostly not vulgar enough to start fights but still pack a little pepper— perfect when you need an easy way to express frustration with a more poetic air than simple damns and shits.

CZECH
Kokotina!
"Bullshit!"
> Derived from *kokot*, the word for rooster/cock.

FINNISH
Mitä helvettiä?
"What the hell fuck?"

GERMAN
Mowendreck!
"Seagull shit!"

HUNGARIAN
Fasz kivan!
"The dick is out!"
> This expression implies a gigantic mess, or that trouble is about to begin.

JAPANESE
Chikushou!

"Beast!"

> In Japanese culture, to call someone a *chikushou* is quite an insulting thing, despite the seemingly mild translation.

MONGOLIAN
Huur!

"Carrion!"

> Another culturally specific oath, although it's not nice to call someone carrion in any language.

POLISH
Rany Boskie!

"God's wounds!"

> This common Polish oath is just the ticket for those who want to add some Catholic guilt to their swearing.

PORTUGUESE (BRAZILIAN)
Vai ceifar batatas!

"Go dig potatoes!"

> This phrase basically means "Get lost!"

RUSSIAN
Khren!

"Horseradish!"

> Similar to saying "Bullshit!"

SPANISH (EUROPE)
¡Me cago en la leche!
"I shat in the milk!"

To shit in the milk is to imply a gigantic mistake or screw-up.

¡Vaya al diablo!
"Go to the devil!"

Used to tell someone to get lost.

SPANISH (COLOMBIA)
¡Qué boleta!
"What a ticket!"

This is the equivalent of saying what a pain in the ass.

SPANISH (PERU)
¡Nancy que Berta!

From the term *nada que ver* (nothing to see) this made-up name is uttered as a way of saying "No f'n' way!"

SWEDISH
Helvetes jävla skit!
"Hell's damned shit!"

> This phrase packs its punch by creatively combining three swears into one.

ZULU
Hhayibo!
"Definitely not!"

> A slangy way of saying "Whoa, no f'n' way!"

WITH RICE OR WITHOUT: A STUDY IN SHEIßE

The German word for shit, *Sheiße* (pronounced *shy-ze*) is the foundation for a diverse collection of curses and exclamations. Although there are other workaday swears, the versatility of *Sheiße* is impressive. It is the Bordeaux of curses, a fine vintage that goes well with everything. Including, apparently, rice.

Scheiße mit Reis!
"Shit with rice!"

> Equivalent of saying "Damn it all to hell!" If you were literally eating shit with your rice, you'd probably utter a harsher profanity. Along the same lines, the Germans also say "Nonsense with sauce!" (*Quatsch mit Soße!*) to mean bullshit/no way/that's stupid. *Quatschkopf* is the term for a talkative idiot.

Sheiße dich aus!
"Go take a shit!"

Sheiße bringt Gluck.
"Shit brings luck."

Sheißfreundlich.
"Shit-friendly."

> To be falsely and excessively friendly.

Sheißeladen.
"Shit-store."
> A shithole, dump, mess.

Sheiße bauen.
"To build shit."
> To screw up.

Sheißdreck!
"Shit dreck!"
> Complete bullshit.

Sheiß machen.
"To make shit/fool around."
> A useful related phrase: *Mach keinen Sheiß!* ("Stop making shit!")

Sheiße drauf!
"Go shit on it!"
> Forget it.

Chapter Three

THE WORLD'S BEST
IDIOMATIC INSULTS
AND OATHS

—⊗⊗⊗—

WHILE SWEARING SHOWS US how we're all alike, it also shows us how we're all different. Every region of the world offers its own unique expletives. America has cocksuckers; Argentina, sock-suckers. French swears invoke pigs; Romanian, pigweed. In Iran, a verbal fart might be directed at a beard; in Greece, at an egg. Other countries' expletives incorporate watermelons, carp, and sesame seeds. It's a gorgeous multicultural mishmash. Oh, the beauty of it all.

The phrases that follow are suited for a wide range of occasions. Some are sayings to encourage your friends to drink more booze (or less booze), and some are ways to call bullshit. Others are elaborate, culturally specific insults or idiomatic oaths of surprise, dismay, or frustration. Others sound like something that a warrior of old would say before entering the fray. Still others offer excellent ways to say that you need to regurgitate your meal, or that someone's fly is open. Some will need no explanation, others could have entire books written about them.

Here are the best we have been able to dig up, arranged by language.

$#@*! $#@*! #$@%! *#@$! $#@! $#@*! $#@! $#@! @#$*! $#@*! $#@! $#@*!

ARABIC
Inta naayim wa rijleek bish-shamis!
"You are asleep and your legs are burning in the sun!"
>Or: You are a fool!

BULGARIAN
Ako šte túrsko da stáne!
"Not even if the Turkish yoke was reimposed!"
>The short translation of this phrase is "Never!" The longer explanation is that the Turks conquered Bulgaria in 1396 and ruled it for five hundred years, and by the commonality of this expression, it would seem that the Bulgarians are still pretty upset about it.

CHINESE (MANDARIN)
Dài lǜmàozi!
"You wear a green hat!"
>Green hats were worn by brothel workers in medieval China, so to say that someone wears a green hat is to imply cuckoldry.

Rǔ xiù wèi gān.
"The smell of milk is not gone from you."
>In other words: you are young and inexperienced.

Sha ji yan yong niu dao!
"You moved house and forgot to take your wife!"
>A man who would move and forget to bring his wife is indeed quite stupid.

On n'a pas elevé les cochons ensemble!

"We didn't raise pigs together!"

> A colleague criticizes your work, a friend questions your driving route, a stranger tries to stop you from walking up the down escalator. You reply with: *On n'a pas elevé les cochons ensemble!* Meaning: What business is it of yours?

Tailler un costard à quelqu'un.

"To cut someone's suit."

> The implication here is that the suit was cut behind one's back, basically, trash-talking.

GERMAN

Stubenhocker!

"Room-sitter!"

> To be a room-sitter in German is to be a boring, useless homebody.

Fruchtchen!

"Little fruit!"

> This implies a good-for-nothing. "Fruit" doesn't carry any homosexual overtones in German.

Radfahrer!

"Bicycle-rider!"

> For Germans, a *radfahrer* is a kiss-ass.

Me pordés avgá de váfontai.

"You can't dye eggs with farts."

> There is nothing that is not true in
> the above expression. You truly
> cannot dye eggs with farts, no matter
> how hard you might try. Those who
> attempt such a useless endeavor are
> clearly lacking in even the most basic
> level of common sense.

Rávdos en ti̱ go̱nía, ára vréchei.

"A walking stick in the corner, therefore it rains."

> In Greek culture, when someone is talking utter nonsense, it
> is best to confront their absurdity head-on with your own
> nonsensical phrase. They will then be forced to compare their
> own faulty reasoning with yours and see the error of their ways.

Lech chapes me yenaaneh otcha!

"Go look for someone to shake you up!"

> According to some native speakers, this Hebrew expression is
> actually quite harsh, despite the mild-sounding translation—the
> English equivalent would be "Go look for somebody to fuck you."

Eveal mashrish!

"Rooting dumb-ass!"

> Perhaps the most poetic expression in this book, we have all met
> someone for whom this term applies—a thoroughly entrenched,
> spectacularly numbskulled dumb-ass.

Ve achotcha hatzolat!

". . . and your limping sister!"

> There is no better way to cut an unpleasant conversation short than with this delightful phrase.
>
> "I'm going to beat the crap out of you!"
>
> "Yeah? You and your limping sister!"

HINDI (INDIA)
Teri behen ka lavda rubber ka!

"Your sister has a rubber dick!"

> All research has shown that the sister is particularly prone to insult, as this colorful and vulgar insult illustrates.

ICELANDIC
Ég borga bara með reiðufé!

"I only pay you with an angry sheep!"

> To begrudgingly do something is to pay with angry sheep.

Nú duga engin vettlingatök!

"Mitten-grabbing will not do!"

> Mitten-grabbing: being an indecisive fool. There is nothing more foolish than mitten-grabbing.

INDONESIAN
Seperti kacang lupa akan kulitnya!

"You're a peanut that's forgotten its shell!"

> This works on two levels: one, you're calling someone a peanut, and two, you're implying that they've forgotten their roots.

Nyamuk mati, gatal tak lepas.

"The mosquito dies but the itch remains."

> This is the kind of thing you say to an old enemy. The insults and trials of the past have faded, but the mutual hatred remains. Then, you draw your swords.

Che attaccabottoni!

"What a button-holer!"

> Long-winded. Boring. Never stops talking.
> In short, a button-holer.

Hai una lingua piena di peli!

"You have a tongue full of hair!"

> Due to your constant sycophantic behavior, your tongue has grown a beard.

Hitori zumoo o totta!

"Like a one-man sumo match!"

> Even more difficult to achieve than a one-man tennis match, a one-man sumo wrestling match is, of course, impossible.

Gomasuri!

"Sesame-seed grinder!"

> You know that guy in your office who only seems work when the boss is watching? The guy whose mess you're always cleaning up and who never gets blamed for any of the problems he causes? That guy is a complete *gomasuri*.

Manaita no ue no koi!
"Like carp on the cutting board!"
>If you, or someone you know, is like carp on the cutting board, we express our sincerest condolences, as you are without a doubt, doomed.

KANNADA (INDIA)
Tunne hidi maneg nadi!
"Hold your dick and go home!"
>Another fairly straightforward insult that gets the job done.

KOREAN
Cho-ding!
"Elementary school student!"
>In other words, a simpleton.

Nam Dae Moon!
"The South Gate of Seoul is open!"
>In this case, the South Gate of Seoul, a historical landmark, is referring to the fly of your trousers, which is open.

LATIN
Lusus naturae!
"Sport of nature!"
>To be a sport of nature is to be a freak.

Nemo me impune lacessit!
"No one provokes me with impunity!"
>This is the ancient motto of the kings of Scotland, but it's quite a thing to say to an enemy.

Nullius filius!
"Bastard!"
>Literally: no man's son.

Har du røyka sokka dine?

"Have you been smoking your socks?"

  Are you mad?

Få ut fingeren av ræva!

"Get the finger out of your ass!"

PERSIAN

Gooz-beh rishet!

"A fart to your beard!"

  To wish a fart upon a Persian man's beard is just as unpleasant
  as it sounds. It is a doubly unpleasant insult to wish a fart upon a
  Persian *woman's* beard.

Glimet ro as ab dar bekesh biroon!

"Pull your carpet out of the water!"

  Taking care of one's rug (in Persian tradition, the most important
  part of a home) is just common sense. Failure to do so would result
  in ridicule and scorn and the general sense in the community that
  you are an idiot.

Hendoone zire baghalam nazaa!

"Don't put watermelon under my arms!"

  Who doesn't like watermelon? They are refreshing and tasty, and to
  be granted a watermelon under each arm would be a wonderful gift
  indeed. But be wary! Perhaps they aren't watermelons under your
  arms after all, but simply the flattering lies of a false friend.

POLISH
Nudne jak flaki z olejem!
"Dull as tripe in oil!"

> A more sensible refrain might be "as revolting as tripe in oil," but in Polish thought, tripe in oil is an exceedingly boring dish.

Raz na ruski rok!
"Once in a Russian year."

> This phrase, meaning "once in a blue moon," or "never," is clearly left over from the bureaucratic nightmare of Soviet rule.

PORTUGUESE
Bunda mole!
"Soft buttocks!"

> Soft buttocks are no good for many reasons, not the least of which is an implication, in Portuguese-speaking countries, that soft-buttocked people are cowards.

Vai pentear macacos!
"Go comb a monkey's hair!"

> In other words: go do something, anything, other than bother me.

Vigarista!
"Like a vicar!"

> "Like a vicar" means not to be religious and authoritative, but, somewhat profanely, to be a swindler.

Pe dinafară trandafir, pe dinăuntru borş cu ştir!

"On the outside, you're a rose, on the inside, you're borscht with pigweed!"

> Borscht is a traditional Slavic soup, prized for being both wholesome and delicious. Borscht with pigweed, however, would be a bitter, acidic slop unfit for consumption by human beings.

Paşte, murgule, iarbă verde!

"Graze, oh bay roan, on green grass!"

> This phrase sounds lovely and poetic, but is in fact a very roundabout way to tell somebody to get lost.

Kak ob st'enku gorokh!

"Like throwing peas against the wall!"

> A useless, impossible task.

Faigh do latha fhein air!

"Get your own day on!"

> The Scots are big ones for revenge, and that's what getting your own day means.

Tiempo a tragar el sapo.

"Time to swallow the toad."

> Even outside of circus tents and extreme eating competitions, toad-swallowing happens every day. We don't want to go to work, or pay our taxes, or nod politely while the crazy person at the bus stop screams at us, but we have no choice. We must swallow the toad.

Tengo que llamar a Hugo!

"I need to call Hugo!"

> We are not exactly certain why "calling Hugo" has come to mean vomiting in Argentina, but it might have something to do with the way a long, drawn out "Hugo" sounds in Spanish: "whooooo-gohh-hhaaa!" It feels good just to say it.

Chupamedias!

"Sock sucker!"

> Some cultures lick boots, others kiss ass. Sycophantic Argentineans are said to suck socks.

SPANISH (EUROPE)

Da un beso a la botella!

"Give the bottle a kiss!"

> This old chestnut does not imply a forced romantic connection with glassware, but to "have another drink, old friend!"

A otro perro con ese hueso!

"Take that bone to another dog!"

> Bullshit artists, con men, and blabbermouths are a dime a dozen in this world. The Spanish, in their wisdom, developed this phrase to command such people to go bother someone else.

Con toda la barba!

"With all of the beard!"

> No man is complete without a long, fulsome, and bushy beard. Therefore, if something— a movie, a meal, a used car—has all of the beard, it is complete, perfect, great.

Atekaye maji mtoni asitukane mamba.

"One who draws water at the river shouldn't curse the crocodile."

> After watching someone shoot themselves in the foot, either literally or figuratively, this phrase is a perfect capper.

Kufa kwa mkundu mavi hutawanyika.

"The death of the anus scatters shit."

> Scatological, yes. But it is an effective way to deride fair-weather friends and hangers-on.

Järnvägar!

"Railways!"

> Notwithstanding any modern person's understandable frustration with the state of the railroad industry, this common oath is a euphemism for *Jävlar!*, which means "Damn!"

Gå som katten kring het gröt.

"To go like a cat around hot porridge."

> To dillydally, to be unnecessarily nervous.

Det var skit att int dynga räckte över hela tegen!

"Shit! Not enough dung for the whole field!"

> Sometimes, even the best and most polite one of us farts at an inappropriate time. To make jest of it, the Swedes say this little phrase.

Ying kratai
"Shoot the rabbit."
>To "shoot the rabbit" is to urinate in public.

TAMIL (INDIA)
Tenga thalayan!
"Coconut-headed one!"
>Trust us, this sounds worse in Tamil than
it does in English.

TURKISH
Bir avuç toprak olmak!
"Become a handful of soil!"

Ecel şerbeti içmek!
"Drink the sherbet of fate!"
>This a very nice-sounding way to tell someone
to go to hell, whose fires, presumably, would make
the sherbet of fate quite refreshing.

Fransiz kalmak.
"To stay like a Frenchman."
>In Turkish culture, a Frenchman does not know
when to leave a party.

Chapter Four

ANIMALS AROUND the WORLD

❧

*A*S CHARLES DARWIN SAID, "Animals, whom we have made our slaves, we do not like to consider our equal." It stands to reason then that almost every culture has insults that equate our enemies to animals. The particularly vilified animal changes from culture to culture, but certain obvious standouts are globally understood: dirty pigs, fat cows, ill-tempered snakes, thick-headed donkeys.

We've included all the standard animal insults in the following pages, along with a few more colorful, hard-to-categorize idioms and expressions from around the globe.

$#@*! $#@*! #$@%! *#@$! $#@! $#@*! $#@! $#@! @#$*! $#@*! $#@! $#@*!

TO THE DOGS

Our canine friends may be loyal, loving companions, but they also eat their own feces and sniff each other's butts. Here is a multicultural kennel of dog insults.

LANGUAGE	Phrase	Translation
ALBANIAN	*Kak oudelic shoon!*	You shit-eating dog!
ARABIC	*Ibn kalb!*	Son of a dog!
ARABIC	*Bint kalb!*	Daughter of a dog!
CZECH	*Syn psa!*	Son of a dog!
DUTCH	*Kankerhond!*	Cancer-dog!
FRENCH	*Tête de chien!*	Dog-face!
FRENCH	*Quelle chienne de vie!*	Life's a bitch!
GERMAN	*Dreckhund!*	Filthy dog!
HINDI	*Paagal kutha!*	Mad dog!
INDONESIAN	*Anjing kurap!*	Ringworm-infested street dog!
ITALIAN	*Brutto cane!*	Butt-ugly dog!
ITALIAN	*Cani e porci!*	Dogs and pigs! (An expression which means everyone without discrimination, i.e., "the place was packed with dogs and pigs!")
JAVANESE	*Djancuk!*	You fucking dog!
SPANISH	*¡Hueles a mierda perro!*	You smell like dog shit!
TAGALOG	*Tae pagkain aso!*	Shit-eating dog!

LANGUAGE	*Phrase*	**Translation**
TURKISH	*Altmış köpeklerin Siz babası!*	You father of sixty dogs!
TURKISH	*Kancik!*	Dog bitch!
UKRAINIAN	*Syn sobaky!*	Son of a dog!
VIETNAMESE	*Thằng chó đẻ!*	Son of a dog!

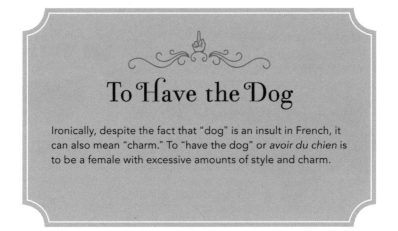

To Have the Dog

Ironically, despite the fact that "dog" is an insult in French, it can also mean "charm." To "have the dog" or *avoir du chien* is to be a female with excessive amounts of style and charm.

COWS

Almost universally, "cow" is used to describe a woman who is large, sluggish, and thick-headed. While not nice in any language, this seems to be an especially popular insult in Eastern European countries, though anyone who's ever watched Soviet bloc women's Olympic sports will be baffled as to why this particular insult should be directed toward the Slavic lands' delicate ladyfolk.

LANGUAGE	*Dumb cow!*
AFRIKAANS	*Dom koei!*
CATALAN	*Vaca tonta!*
CROATIAN	*Nijem krava!*
CZECH	*Hloupá kráva!*
DANISH	*Dumme ko!*
DUTCH	*Domme koe!*
FINNISH	*Tyhmä lehmä!*
FRENCH	*Vache bête!*
GERMAN	*Dumme Kuh!*
HUNGARIAN	*Hülye tehén!*
ITALIAN	*Vacca muto!*
NORWEGIAN	*Dumme ku!*
POLISH	*Krowa!*
PORTUGUESE	*Vaca burra!*
ROMANIAN	*Mut vacă!*
RUSSIAN	*Korova!*

LANGUAGE	*Dumb cow!*
SERBIAN	*Glupa krava!*
SPANISH	*¡Vaca tonta!*
TAGALOG	*Pipi baka!*
UKRAINIAN	*Nimyỹ korovy!*
YIDDISH	*Behaimeh!*

$#@!

Fun Cow Fact

In Mandarin Chinese, young people use the vulgar term "cow's cunt!" to say "That's fucking awesome!" *Niu be!*

DONKEYS

In Arabic and other East Asian cultures, calling someone a donkey (or a descendant of a donkey) is a vile insult. Although donkeys carry the implication of being thickheaded and stubborn, this insult goes beyond such characteristics, as Islamic tradition considers donkeys to be impure animals. In the Koran, it is said that if someone is at prayer, and a dog or a donkey passes by them, their prayers are annulled, and the braying of a donkey indicates that the animal has been visited by Satan.

Donkey!

ARABIC
Hemaar!

HINDI
Gadhā!

PERSIAN
Khar!

TURKISH
Eşek!

Son of a Donkey!

ARABIC
Ibn il-hemaar!

HINDI
Gadha da khurr!

PERSIAN
Kor-e khar!

TURKISH
Eşşoğlu eşek!

In some situations, amongst family members, for instance, the Arabic phrase for "little donkey" (*jahsh*) can be used affectionately.

PIGS

∽

Unsavory sausage makers have often been said to use "everything but the squeal" in their wares. The same can be said of pig-based insults and idioms, as they are as rich and as full as a well-packed kielbasa. However, unlike sausage, pig insults are not as useful in paella.

GERMAN
Du alte Sau!
"You dirty pig!"

Die Saubande!
"You pack of filthy swine!"

ITALIAN
Sei uno vero porco!
"You are a real pig!"
> In Italian youth slang, *porco* tends to denote a sexual pervert, whereas most other languages use pig simply to mean fat and slovenly.

YIDDISH
A chazzer bleibt a chazzer!
"Once a pig, always a pig!"
> This Yiddish proverb doubles as a handy insult.

Fat Pigs

ALBANIAN
Derr pista!

Fun German Pig Fact 1:

Germans use either *Schwein* (swine) or *Sau* (sow) for their pig insults. We've all heard the antique insult *Schweinhund* (pig-dog), but that's not really used by modern Germans.

Fun German Pig Fact 2:

In the face of something remarkable or surprising, Germans utter *Mein Schwein pfeift!* "My pig's whistling!"

FRENCH
Tu gros porc!

ICELANDIC
Þú feitur svín!

NORWEGIAN
Du feit gris!

SPANISH
¡Chancha!

SWAHILI
Wewe mafuta nguruwe!

VIETNAMESE
Bạn mỡ lợn!

THE ANIMAL KINGDOM

Animals can swim, fly, and poop on the living room carpet, but they cannot swear. Fortunately, the international language of profanity has seen fit to include them in many of its phrases, so they need not feel left out. These insults, rich with metaphor, language puns, vulgarity, and wit, say more about the human condition than they do about the animal kingdom. Perhaps we are the true animals after all.

AFRIKAANS
Bakvissie!
"Goldfish!"
> In South African slang, a goldfish is a silly-minded teenage girl.

ARABIC
Bahaayim!
"Livestock!"
> This Arabic insult can be used towards any large group of uncouth idiots (football fans, mall shoppers, highway drivers).

CHINESE (CANTONESE)
Yín chóng!
"Lewd worm!"
> A lewd worm is a man who frequents brothels, or more generally a lecher.

CZECH
Pasák!
"Sheep-herder!"
> With this animal-based insult, you are basically calling someone a pimp.

DUTCH
Angsthaas!

"Fear-hare!"

Rabbits usually connote sexual promiscuity, but in Dutch, you call a coward a fear-hare.

GERMAN
Sumpfralle!

"Swamp-rail bird!"

A swamp-rail is a bird that lives in, naturally, the swamp. It is considered dirty and unattractive, so to call someone a *Sumpfralle* is to call them ugly.

HINDI
Ullu!

"Owl!"

In Hindi, calling someone an "owl" does not connote wisdom as it does in English, but instead dimwitted ignorance.

ICELANDIC
Þorski!

"Cod!"

A cod, in Iceland, is a simpleminded fool. This same insult works in Italian: *Merluzzo!*

KOREAN
Daegori!

"Chicken-headed!"

This insult is generally used in genuine anger, despite how soft it sounds.

$#@!

Bird Person

As we've seen with the grass mud horse, Chinese swearing often involves language puns. In Mandarin, the word *niao* means "bird," but rhymes with the word for "penis." Creative Chinese cursers have developed a whole slew of inventive *niao* puns, which over time have turned the word *niao* into a euphemism for "fuck."

Woniaoni!
"Fuck you!"

Niaohua!
Literally "bird talk," but with the pun, it means "fucking words" or bullshit.

Niaoren!
"Bird person" (fucking asshole).

PERSIAN
Zahr e maar!
"Poison of the snake!"

> This exclamation can be used towards someone as an insult (meaning they have the poison of the snake) or just as a general oath of anger and frustration. It's especially useful when someone is giving you grief.

PORTUGUESE
Cara de fuinha!
"Ferret-face!"

> Used to describe an ugly person, weak-chinned and narrow faced.

RUSSIAN
Krysa!
"Rat!"

> This is a very common Russian insult that has exactly the meaning you'd think: a vile, dirty, untrustworthy person.

SPANISH (ARGRENTINA)
¡Guacho!/¡Guacha!
"Hey, ya bastard!"

> In Argentina, this is a genial way to call somebody an SOB or a bastard; its literal meaning is that of a small animal that has been left alone in the wilderness without parents.

Monkeys

In Arabic and East Asian cultures, monkey insults (like monkeys themselves) are common.

ARABIC
Qerd!
"Monkey!"
> In Arabic, to call someone a monkey, you shout *Tiizak hamra!* ("Your ass is red!") Monkeys apparently have red asses, so there you go.

HINDI
Baander!
"Monkey!"

INDONESIAN
Budak monyet bodoh!
"Stupid slave monkey!"

SPANISH (MEXICO)

¡Güey!

"Ox!"

> The word *güey* literally means ox or steer, but in common slang it has come to mean "dude."

THAI

Kwai!

"Stupid buffalo!"

> The buffalo is the go-to animal for Thai insults.

YIDDISH

Alter bok!

"Old goat!"

> This is a great thing to call a stubborn old man.

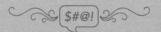

Dead Hens and Black Hens

Galinha morta—a Brazilian Portuguese term that basically means dumb-ass or worthless—is often used when fans are dumbstruck by a terrible play in football:

> *Maradona nem chegou perto da bola. Uma verdadeira galinha morte!*
> "Maradona didn't even get near the ball. A real dead chicken!"

In Brazil, much scorn is heaped on Argentina's legendary footballer Diego Maradona, who suffered from drug addiction and obesity after retirement. Brazilians call him "fatty," or *gordo*. This moniker (the same word in both Spanish and Portuguese) is an affectionate nickname for Maradona in Argentina and other Spanish-speaking countries, but on Internet chat boards, Brazilians often deride Maradona as a "hamburger-eater," a *hambúrgueres*.

A black hen, or *galinha preta*, is a euphemism for bad luck. Acting like a hen or *galinhagem* is shorthand for being a pervert.

Chapter Five

CURSES
AND
MALEDICTIONS

∞

B ACK BEFORE THE WRITTEN WORD and literacy were common aspects of civilization, the power of speech reigned supreme. The verbal curse—less a vulgar insult than a supplication to the heavens to cause harm and ill to another person—was the preferred way to cast aspersion, register disproval, and display righteous anger.

The art of the curse ranges from simple commands to die to intricate and creative wishes for misfortune, bodily harm, and gruesome violence to befall the accursed. Some of these curses have trickled down into our modern world, while others have been updated to suit the twenty-first century. Still others may have vanished from common usage, but the curse remains a fantastic resource for the creative swearer.

$#@*! $#@*! #$@%! *#@$! $#@! $#@*! $#@! $#@! @#$*! $#@*! $#@! $#@*!

DEATH AND DISMEMBERMENT

Death curses, blunt and to the point, are common to all cultures. Some go straight for the jugular, while others take more creative paths to invoke the accursed's demise.

Death by Violence

LITHUANIAN
Kad tave zeme prarytu!
"May the earth swallow you!"

NIGERIAN
Egbe gbarie kwa gi isi!
"May a gun blow your head off!"

Sudden Painful Death

ARABIC
Yaatak darba fi 'albak!
"I hope your heart gets hit!"

FINNISH
Kuse muuntajaan!
"May you piss into a transformer!"
    In other words: electrocution.

GREEK (ANCIENT)
Diarregeies!
"May you burst!"

SERBIAN
Da bi te majka prepoznala u bureku!
"May your mother recognize you in a meat pie!"
> That is to say, stuffed through a meat grinder.

YIDDISH
A feier zol im trefen!
"May you burn up!"

Epic Death

GUJARTI (INDIA)
Taru nakkhod jai!
"May destruction befall you!"

SCOTTISH
Mile marbhphaisg ort!
"A thousand death shrouds upon you!"

Simply Drop Dead

CHINESE (CANTONESE)
Puk gai!
> Literally means falling into the street, but the curse implies "May you die in the street and be left to rot since no one, not even your family, cares to pick you up!"

JAPANESE
Shinjimae!
"May you drop dead!"

FAMILY CURSES

Sending holy damnation down upon an entire family is a signature element of old-world curses. It extends the insult both up and down the family tree. There's a tang of anger to these curses that—even to the modern ear—makes them seem wholeheartedly vicious.

ARABIC
Yikhrib
"May God destroy your house and the house of those who gave birth to you!"

Allaah yiljan abu ommak!
"May God curse your dead grandfather!"

CHINESE (CANTONESE)
Ham gaa caan!
"May your whole family be dead!"

CYPRIOT
Gamo tin havra sou he ton kapike sou!
"Damn your family and its place of origin!"

SERBIAN
Da bog da trazio detzoo Gaygerovim broyachem!
"May God grant that you search for your children with a Geiger counter!"

SPANISH
¡Me cago en tus muertos!
"I shit on your dead family!"

Financial Curses

In many cultures, it is rude to discuss money. It is even ruder to use any of the phrases that follow, curses that wish financial ruin on the recipient. Use them with care. In the words of the esteemed RuPaul: "Don't let your mouth write a check your ass can't cash."

HINDI
Apa eka sau betiyam haim mai!
"May you have a hundred daughters!"
> The curse here does not relate to the discomfort of a hundred childbirths, but rather to the financial pain that will arise from having to supply a costly marriage dowry for a hundred brides.

SERBIAN
Dada ti zena rodila stonogu pa ceo zivot radio za cipele!
"May your wife give birth to a centipede so you have to work to buy shoes all your life!"

THE IRISH: KINGS OF THE COLORFUL CURSE

The Irish language has long been lauded for its lyrical qualities, and the list of impressive poets and writers of Irish origin further attests to the fact that "the gift of the gab" is more than just a cliché. Trickling down through ancient songs and stories, and often updated and adapted, this collection of Irish curses (in old and modern Irish) demonstrate the creative cursing power of the Irish.

Narab marthain duit!
"May you not remain alive!"

Go n-ithe an cat thú, is go n-ithe an diabhal an cat.
"May the cat eat you, and may the devil eat the cat."

Imeacht gan teacht ort!
"May you leave without returning!"

Dolma n-aithisc for fer th'inaid do grés.
"Hesitant speech on your successors forever."
    This one is particularly painful for a culture
    known for its eloquence.

Gura féis ic faelaib do chorp!
"May your body be a feast for wolves!"

Dá n-ó pill fort!
"Two horses' ears upon you!"

Dóite agus loisceadh ort!
"A burning and a scorching upon you!"

Bad nenaid co bráth a lucht!
"May this household be nettles forever!"

Ní raib úaid acht cairem círmaire nó nech bed fíu iad!
"May none spring forth from you but shoemakers and comb-makers and their like!"

Beirid tríst mallachta in nóem néerenn!
"May they bear the curses of all the saints of Ireland!"

Gurab bás do rinn nosbéra!
"May it be by spear-point that death takes him!"

Mo mallacht is mallacht ríg nime ar lín in tighi-sea i tái!
"My curse and the curse of the king of heaven upon all those within your house!"

Gurab écen mér dot múnad in airecht!
"May you become so insignificant that it be necessary to point you out by finger in a crowd!"

RELIGIOUS AND PROFANE CURSES

While asking God to strike someone down is a surprisingly common insult, there are plenty of other more baroque and interesting profane curses, most of them mixing the scatological with the sacred for shock value. Telling someone that you will shit on them is bad enough, but to say that God will shit on them, or that you will shit on God, ends up carrying a lot of weight, curse-wise.

European cultures steeped in Catholicism, like Spain and Italy, are experts at profane cursing. In Spain, *hostia*, referring to the sacramental host (the bread taken at communion), is used in various sacrilegious exclamations. If someone says of you, *no tener media hostia*, they are saying you don't have half a host, meaning you're an utter weakling.

Swearing upon the host's whore, *¡Hostia puta!* is a common vulgar exclamation.

Italians seem to have taken this form of cursing to its utter extremis. Profane, sexual, and scatological—these curses all sound like something Linda Blair might've shouted in *The Exorcist*, but we've been assured that in Italian, these are not nearly as shocking sounding. But perhaps our sources are just gleefully waiting for us to use them in public.

Porco Dio!
"God is a filthy pig!"

Dio cane!
"God is a dog!"

Dio merda!
"God is shit!"

Dio inculato!
"God has been fucked!"

Madonna puttana!
"The Virgin Mary is a whore!"

Vacca Madonna!
"Virgin Mary is a stupid cow!"

Porca Madonna!
"The Virgin Mary is a filthy pig!"

Mannaggia Cristo!
"Bloody Jesus Christ!"

Puttana Eva!
"Eve is a whore!"

Porco Dio, porca Madonna e tutti gli angeli in colonna!
"Fuck that filthy pig God, the Holy Mother, and all the angels in line!"

Of a somewhat milder nature, French Canadians often curse the Tabernacle (meaning the Church).

Maudit batard tabarnak!
"Damn bastard Tabernacle!"

> *Tabernak!* can also be used as an insult towards someone, *Tabernak de toi!* basically meaning "Fuck you!" *Tabernak* also appears in the phrase "Who the fuck cares?" (*On s'en tabarnaque!*)

ILLNESS AND OTHER UNPLEASANTRIES

When wishing death is too good for someone, we turn to horrible illnesses and vulgar sex acts to add some spice to our insults. These curses all have a modern flair to them, but are direct descendants of an older cursing tradition.

The Dutch are considered experts in this form of swearing. In fact, almost *all* of the Netherlands' swear words are focused on disease. Looking at the amazing quantity of Dutch illness insults, average human beings tend to at first be stunned, then amused, then offended, and then finally amused again. And then offended again. It's a slippery, disease-ridden slope. These insults are so commonplace in Dutch culture that the apparent vulgarity has been watered down—much like celebrity dancing competitions, the common public has become inured to their offensive qualities.

Krijg de typhus!
"May you go get typhus!"

Krijg de takke!
"May you go have a stroke!"

Krijg het lazarus!
"May you go catch leprosy!"

Krijg de vliegende vinkentering!
"Catch the flying-finch tuberculosis!"

This preoccupation with disease has created a whole brand of insults relating to telling people they are ill:

Pestkop!
"Plague-head!"

Kankermongool!
"Cancer-mongoloid!"

Pleurislijer!
"Tuberculosis-sufferer!"

Klerelijer!
"Cholera-sufferer!"

Takkewijf!
"Stroke-woman!"

Vulgar Sexual Curses

Mean-spirited? Check. Vulgar? Check. Inappropriate? Check. Profane? Check. These insults shouldn't be used in any situation where you would like to make friends, defuse a tense situation, or not get punched in the mouth. These are the kind of thing very bad twelve-year-old boys say and then giggle. Anyone older than that using these terms had better watch their step.

ALBANIAN
Te qifte arusha qorre!
"May you be raped by a blind bear!"

ARABIC
Elif air ab dinikh!
"A thousand dicks in your religion!"

ARMENIAN
Krisnera zhazh tan vred!
"May the rats ejaculate on you!"

BULGARIAN
Gladna Karpatska valchitza s dalag kosam minet da ti prai deeba!
"May you be fucked by a Carpathian she-wolf!"

SERBIAN
Jebo te Papa!
"May the Pope fuck you!"

Chapter Six

FIGHTING WORDS

᠆᠆᠆᠆᠆

A COMMONLY HEARD REFRAIN before one travels abroad is "Remember, you are an ambassador for your country." In other words, tread lightly, be courteous, observe local customs, and treat all those you meet with respect. This is both a prescription for good manners and helpful advice for life in general. However, there are times when, against all better judgment, you may wish to throw politeness and courtesy out the window and behave abysmally toward your newfound enemies and anyone else within earshot.

Within this chapter you will find some of the rudest and most vile put-downs and insults ever dreamed of by the human race. Using any of these is sure to cause you to be spit upon, slapped, or worse, so be prepared.

$#@*! $#@*! #$@%! *#@$! $#@! $#@*! $#@! $#@! @#$*! $#@*! $#@! $#@*!

PUTTING THE "YOU" IN "FUCK YOU!"

‿✑

It's impossible to swear in Japanese. Or so know-it-alls at cocktail parties are fond of saying. What they mean is that in the Japanese language, there are no specifically "taboo" words; by themselves, there is no such thing as a "bad" Japanese word. The same is often said of many Native American languages.

There might not be any social constraints that relate specifically to language (that is, Japanese has no "naughty" words) but that doesn't mean there aren't plenty of rude and offensive things to say— especially when contrasted with the very polite and class-conscious mannerisms of Japanese society.

For instance, even the word "you" can be a swear word in Japan. Just as in French or other Romance languages, Japanese has many subtle ways of saying "you." The most insulting is sort of a sarcastically polite "you" that the Japanese consider extremely rude.

Ki sama.
"Oh precious sir."
> While it translates as "Oh precious sir" it is more like saying, "Oh, precious sir, you are a complete fucking bastard."

You can use *ki sama* on its own as an insult, or add it to other insulting phrases:

Ki sama, namen janeyo!
"Hey you piece-of-shit bastard, don't fuck with me!"

A less insulting, but still offensive form of "you" is *temee*. This is often translated as "bastard."

Remember, however, these words don't literally mean bastard, or asshole, they just mean "you."

Another surefire way to hurl a deadly serious insult in Japanese is to cast aspersions upon someone's status. Calling someone a hick is incredibly rude.

Imo yaro!
"Potato guy!"
> This would be the equivalent of calling someone an "an inbred piece of poor white trash" in English.

Imo ne-chan!
"Potato-sister!"
> Use this for the female hick.

Other insulting Japanese phrases:

Bakayaro!
"Idiot!"
> This catchall Japanese insult literally translates as "idiot," but is much harsher than the English word. *Bakayaro* can be shortened to *Baka!* for a quick jolt of ill-will.

Using any of these terms towards someone might prompt them to command, *Keri o tsuke yoze!* ("Let's take this outside!")

IF THE SHOE FITS AND THE MOUSTACHE GROWS

Shoes and moustaches are the double-edged sword of Arabic cursing.

In Arabic cultures, swearing "upon my moustache" is a quite a serious thing to do. Iraqis have been known to seal business deals on a moustache, and lavishing praise on a man's facial hair is the utmost compliment. Conversely, insulting a moustache is a sure way to show scorn and disrespect.

Sala shawarbi!
"Upon my moustache!"

In 2003, an Iraqi envoy insulted his Kuwaiti counterpart at a summit meeting by telling him "Shut up, you monkey! Curses be upon your moustache!" The meeting, we can assume, devolved from there.

At the opposite end from the mighty moustache, the shoe is considered filthy and impure, so to throw a shoe at someone or to place a shoe upon someone's head is to imply that they are worthless and lower than human. Shoe insults are usually reserved for extreme situations (the toppled statues of Saddam Hussein were attacked with shoes after his fall from power).

Here are a few shoe insults:

Ya gazma yibn ig-gazma!
"You son of a shoe!"

Surmayye a'raasac!
"A shoe upon your head!"

Mokhu gazma!
"His mind is as low and dirty as a shoe!"

Howa jaawiz id-darb bi-sittiin gazma!
"He deserves to be hit with sixty shoes!"

In fact, simply showing the sole of your shoe can be deemed offensive in Arabic culture. This notion of unclean feet is also prevalent in Southeast Asia, where it's considered impolite to cross your legs for fear of accidentally showing someone the sole of your shoe.

VITTU TO YOU!

∽

While the previously mentioned *perkele* is the most celebrated curse in Finnish, *vittu* is the most offensive. Like "cunt" in English, it's the most vulgar way to describe the female genitalia, but unlike its English counterpart, *vittu* has snuck its way into a wide array of insults and expressions, closely mirroring the way English speakers use "fuck" or even milder swear words. Depending on the situation, it can range from mild to very strong and offensive.

Haista vittu!
"Fuck you!"
    The literal translation here is "Smell my cunt!"

Vittu voi!
"Fuck this!"

Mitä vittua?
"What the fuck?"

Meni vituiksi.
"That's fucked up."

Vittu tätä paskaa!
"Fuck this shit!"

Vitun tyhmä!
"You're fucking stupid!"

Vitun mulkku!

"Fucking prick!"

This is particularly funny when you remember what *vittu* really means.

Hevonvittu!

"Horse's cunt!"

Used as English-speakers use "bullshit."

Hevonvitunperse!

"Fucking horse's cunt!"

Vittumainen!

"You dumb fuck!"

This literally means "like a cunt."

Minua vituttaa!

"I am fucking pissed off!"

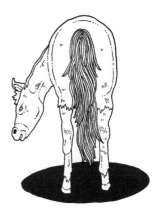

MESS WITH THE BULL, YOU GET THE HORNS . . .

Throughout Europe and especially in Mediterranean countries, "giving someone the horns," or telling someone that they are "horned," is a serious and offensive insult. Being horned is a euphemism for having been cuckolded (said to have arisen during Elizabethan-era comic plays, when a character would wear horns on his head to let the audience know he was a cuckolded dimwitted husband), so it's sort of like saying "Your wife steps out on you!"

LANGUAGE	*Horned one!*
CZECH	*Paroháč!*
FRENCH	*Cocu!*
GREEK	*Keratas!*
HUNGARIAN	*Felszarvazni!*
ITALIAN	*Cornuto!*
PORTUGUESE	*Chifrudo!*
ROMANIAN	*Incornorat!*
RUSSIAN	*Rogonosets!*
SERBIAN	*Rogonia!*
SPANISH	*Cornudo!*
TURKISH	*Boynuzlu!*

In many European cultures, these terms are paired with a horn hand gesture. To perform it, make a fist with the index and pinky fingers extended (like the "rock on" heavy metal sign) and then prepare to run away.

For more internationally flavored offensive gestures, check out our sister book, *Rude Hand Gestures Around the World.*

A WORLD OF F

You're already an expert in the F-word. Now you'll learn the G-word (*Gamato!*), the Y-word (*Yumago!*) and the B-word (*Baszd meg!*). The helpful chart that follows details F-word variants from around the world, from the standard "Fuck off" to the more colorful "Fuck you, slimy monitor lizard!" While not all these words translate as "fuck," these are the terms that translate the best to the harshness of "Fuck you!"

LANGUAGE	Phrase	Translation
CHINESE (CANTONESE)	*Diu nei!*	Fuck you!
CHINESE (MANDARIN)	*Kao bibei!*	Fuck off!
FRENCH	*Casse-toi!*	Fuck off!
GERMAN	*Verpiss dich, Arschloch!*	Fuck off, asshole!
GREEK	*Gamato!*	Fucker!
HINDI (INDIA)	*Bhen chhod bhaynchod!*	Sister-fucker!
HUNGARIAN	*Baszd meg!*	Fuck you!
ICELANDIC	*Naridill!*	Corpse fucker!
ITALIAN	*Vaffanculo!*	Fuck you!
KOREAN	*Yumago!*	Fuck you!
PORTUGUESE	*Foda-se!*	Fuck you!
ROMANIAN	*Du-te dracului!*	Go fuck yourself!
SPANISH	*Vete a la verga!*	Go fuck yourself!
SWEDISH	*Din jävla idiot!*	You fucking idiot!
TAMIL (INDIA)	*Oor othe thevidiya!*	Everyone in the village fucks you!
THAI	*Yet mung ai hee-ah!*	Fuck you, slimy monitor lizard!

Chapter Seven

GLOBAL SCATOLOGY 101 AND NAUGHTY BITS

〰〰〰

C URSING ISN'T ALL INSULTS and put-downs. There's a whole world of vulgar language that relates to our body parts, what we do with those body parts, and all the various fluids that come out of them. There is, of course, plenty of crossover into the land of insults that arises when we talk about body parts and what comes out of them—we'll be sure to catalog those here as well.

$#@*! $#@*! #$@%! *#@$! $#@! $#@*! $#@! $#@! @#$*! $#@*! $#@! $#@*!

NUMBER TWO IS NUMBER ONE

∽

By any other name, it's the shit. While we've already detailed some of the ways to say number two, here's a more comprehensive list fit for those with their minds in the toilet.

Keep in mind that not all of these are used as exclamations the way "Shit!" is used in English—these are just the coarsest ways to say excrement.

LANGUAGE	Shit
AFRIKAANS	*Kak*
ARABIC	*Khara*
BULGARIAN	*Laĭna*
CHINESE (MANDARIN)	*Dà biàn*
CROATIAN	*Govno*
CZECH	*Hovno*
DANISH	*Lort*
DUTCH	*Schijt*
FRENCH	*Merde*
GERMAN	*Scheiße*
GREEK	*Skatá*
HINDI	*Mala*
ICELANDIC	*Sjitturinn*
ITALIAN	*Merda*
JAPANESE	*Kuso*
KOREAN	*Ttong*

LANGUAGE	Shit
LITHUANIAN	Šūdas
NORWEGIAN	Dritt
POLISH	Gówno
PORTUGUESE	Merda
ROMANIAN	Rahat
RUSSIAN	Gavno
SPANISH	Mierda
SWEDISH	Skit
TAGALOG	Tae
THAI	Xu
TURKISH	Bok
UKRANIAN	Layno
VIETNAMESE	Cuc

SCATOLOGICAL EXCLAMATIONS AND INSULTS *OR* HOW TO THROW SHIT

cS∕∂

We've detailed the Germans' delightful use of *Scheiße* and the Spaniards' desire to *cago* upon your dead family, but they aren't the only ones who know their shit. Here are a few more examples from around the world:

ARABIC
Akhra min kida mafiiš.
"There's nothing shittier than this."

CHINESE (CANTONESE)
Hem ga tsan.
"You are a screw-up who would be better off eating shit."

CHINESE (MANDARIN)
Shǐ dàn!
"Shit-egg!"

DUTCH
Schijtluis!
"Shit-louse!"

FRENCH
Quelle merdouille!
"What a shit-scene!"

JAPANESE
Kusottare!
"Shit-leaker!"

POLISH
Ty gnoju!
"You are dung!"

Goh e-ziad nakhor!
"Don't eat excessive amounts of shit!"

PORTUGUESE
Caganita!
"Animal crap!"

ROMANIAN
Ă cac pe tine!
"I shit on you!"

SPANISH (CENTRAL AMERICA)
¡Te cagaste!
"You really shat on yourself!"
    Used ironically to describe a stroke of unintended good luck.

SWEDISH
Ta dig i arslet!
"Go grab your ass!"

Skitstövel!
"Shit-boot!"

XHOSA (AFRICA)
Shrama sakho!
"A skidmark on your underwear!"

THE NAUGHTY BITS

Call them what you will—T&A, the bells and whistle, the special purpose—there are plenty of vulgar and euphemistic terms for the "nether regions." Some are insults, some are affectionate—fitting for the body parts that are the cause of many great pleasures as well as countless complications and *sticky* situations.

CHINESE (MANDARIN)
Mīmī
In China, cats don't meow, they mewl "*mīmī*," which is also a euphemism for a woman's breasts.

Lǎo èr.
"Little brother."
In real life, a little brother can be a source of bother, an annoying little squirt who follows you around and causes grief, but whom—at the end of the day—you have great affection for. In Mandarin, *lǎo èr* (or "little brother") is a euphemism for the penis, but the description above still fits.

Jiào nǐshēng háizi méi pìgu yǎn.
"May your child be born with an imperforate anus."
Best use of "imperforate" in a body-part-related insult.

DUTCH
Klooztak!
Hurl this insult ("*orbsack!*") at a male who is acting particularly dick-ish.

Kut!

This is the female counterpart to the above term. In other words, it's the nastiest way to say the female genitalia. Use with caution, as this is extremely offensive.

FRENCH

Enculer les mooches

The rear end in French is *cul*, which gets us to the colorful French expression *enculer les mouches*, to sodomize flies, which means to quibble or waste time over nothing.

GREEK

Malaka

If you've watched *The Wire*, you know this one, which means "wanker" or chronic masturbator. Formerly a pretty harsh insult, it now can be used affectionately toward your most knuckleheaded friends.

ICELANDIC

Farðu í rassgat!

In Iceland, *rassgat* (asshole) is a popular curse word, and is used in the Icelandic equivalent of "go fuck yourself," literally meaning "go into the asshole."

INDONESIAN

Burung

Literally "bird," but here it means "penis." This gives new, hilarious meaning to the old saying, "a bird in the hand is worth two in the bush."

Un sacco di balle

Meaning "a great sack of balls" ("balls" in the sense of testicles), this is Italian for a load of nonsense.

Figa di legno

An arrogant woman not worth the time to talk to can be said to have a "vagina of wood." The implication here is that she makes herself out to be something she's not.

Una minchiata

In Sicilian Italian slang, a penis is a *minchia*; you therefore can complain about *una minchiata*, which is a penis-like (supremely stupid) situation.

RUSSIAN
Zalupatsia!

In Russian, the penis is the *zalupa*, and if someone is putting on airs or acting arrogant, you can call them *zalupatsia!* (basically, penis-head).

Epilogue
PARTING WORDS

 ✍

Having spent the entirety of this book spreading the gospel of the vulgar, obscene, and insulting, we would be remiss if we didn't leave you with this chart below, which should require no explanation and may perhaps get you out of the hot water your loose tongue has caused.

LANGUAGE	I am sorry
ARABIC	*Ana aasif*
BULGARIAN	*Sãžaljavam*
CHINESE (CANTONESE)	*Deui m' jyu*
CHINESE (MANDARIN)	*Duì bù qı*
DANISH	*Undskyld*
DUTCH	*Het spijt mij*
FRENCH	*Je suis désolé / désolée*
GERMAN	*Es tut mir leid*
GREEK	*Lypámai*
HEBREW	*Ani mitzta'er / mitzta'eret*
HINDI	*Mujhe maph kardo*
HUNGARIAN	*Bocsánat*
ICELANDIC	*Því miður*
INDONESIAN	*Maaf*
ITALIAN	*Vi chiedo scusa*

LANGUAGE	I am sorry
JAPANESE	*Moushiwake arimasen deshita*
KOREAN	*Miyanhamnida*
LITHUANIAN	*Atsiprašau*
NORWEGIAN	*Unn-skyll mei*
PERSIAN	*Bebakhshid*
PORTUGUESE	*Desculpa*
ROMANIAN	*Ertați-mă*
RUSSIAN	*Ya proshu proschenija*
SPANISH	*Lo siento mucho*
SWAHILI	*Amahani*
SWEDISH	*Jag är ledsen*
VIETNAMESE	*Xin lỗi*

ACKNOWLEDGMENTS

A sincere and gracious thank you to the following people for their help in compiling many of the terms discussed in this book. In no particular order, thanks to Susie Ghahremani and her family, Jo Pires-O'Brien, Suzanne LaGasa, Becca Cohen, Marie Oishi, Tomer Hanuka, Kenichi Hoshine, Mu Pan, Kim Du, 金山, Greg Stadler, and Conor Quinn. Additonally, another very big thank-you to Jenny Traig, and to Jennifer Kong, Emily Haynes, and Courtney Drew at Chronicle Books.